LUDWIG VAN BEETHOVEN

SEPTET

for Violin, Viola, Violoncello, Double-bass,
Clarinet, Horn and Bassoon
für Violine, Bratsche, Violoncello, Kontrabaß,
Klarinette, Horn und Fagott
E♭ major / Es-Dur / Mi♭ majeur
Op. 20

Ernst Eulenburg Ltd

London · Mainz · Madrid · New York · Paris · Prague · Tokyo · Toronto · Zürich

BEETHOVEN,
SEPTET IN E FLAT MAJOR, OP. 20

Beethoven's Septet, probably his most popular work, circulated in countless arrangements and later belittled by himself for that very reason, may, in subject matter, be traced back, in part, to the Sextet for 2 Clarinets, 2 Horns and 2 Bassoons— a work belonging to the composer's Bonn period and published as op. 71. Sketches for the Septet date from the year 1799. Originally heard at a private party given by Prince Schwarzenberg, it was publicly performed at one of Beethoven's concerts given on April 2nd 1800 in the Imperial National Court Theatre in Vienna. The announcement of this concert stated that the Septet was dedicated to the Empress Maria Theresia[1]), the second wife of the Emperor Francis II. On December 15th, 1800, the composer offered the work to the publisher Franz Anton Hoffmeister, who, shortly before, had founded the "Bureau de musique" in Leipzig (C. F. Peters since 1814) with the organist Ambrosius Kühnel. In his letter Beethoven designates the individual instruments collectively as obbligato parts, and then continues: "I can write nothing which is not obbligato, as I came into the world myself with an obbligato accompaniment. This Septet has met with great success. For general use, the three wind instruments, Bassoon[2]), Clarinet and Horn can be replaced[3]) by another Violin, another Viola and another Violoncello." On January 15th, 1801, he stipulated that his fee should be 20 ducats, the same sum that he obtained for the first Symphony, op. 21, and the Piano Sonata, op. 22. In June, 1801, he assured his publishers—disconcerted by some rumours—that he had sold this work to nobody else, and added: "Moreover I believe Salomon[4]) is as incapable of the trick of printing the Septet as I am of selling it to him; I am so conscientious, that I have refused various publishers who have asked me for the Piano score of the Septet, and yet I do not know if you yourself can make use of it."

In the same letter Beethoven gave the following title to the Septet, couched in terms which appear odd to us in these days:

Septette

Pour un violon, Viole, violon celle, contre Basse, un cors, une Clarinette, un fagot
composé et dedié

à Sa. Majesté l'imperatrice et Reine
par louis van Beethoven
oeuvre 20.

---

[1]) For this Empress who died in 1807, aged 34, after the birth of her twelfth child, cf. Carl Leeder, Beethoven's Dedications in "Die Musik", Vol. 10 (1904), page 425 etc.

[2]) Note the remarkable arrangement of the corresponding instruments.

[3]) Strangely enough this actual arrangement never appeared; but a transcription of the work for Flute Quintet (Flute, Violin, 2 Violas and Violoncello), transposed into G major, and offered by Beethoven to his Leipzig publisher on April 22nd, 1801, was brought out by Witzendorf of Vienna. "Amateurs of the flute, who have approached me in the matter, will now be glad to swarm over the work like flies, and feed on it", wrote Beethoven in his letter.

[4]) Beethoven had sent the Septet out of friendship to this well known concert director in London, before sending it to Hoffmeister. He did this with a view to having the work performed in London, but with the express injunction that it was not to fall into other hands, as he, Beethoven, wished to have the composition printed in Germany.

On the title page of the original edition in two parts, which does not seem to have appeared before the middle of the year 1802, we read however: "Septetto pour Violon, Alto, Clarinette, Corno, Basson, Violoncelle et Contre-Basse composé et dedié à Sa Majesté Marie Therese, L'Imperatrice romaine, Reine d'Hongrie et de Bohème, etc., etc., par Louis van Beethoven, Oeuvre 20".

On April 8th, 1802, Beethoven pressed his publishers to hurry on with the production of the work, and said: "Send my Septet into the world a bit quicker—for the vulgar are waiting for it, and as you know, the Empress has it—I won't answer for any-thing—there are rogues in the Imperial town as well as at the Imperial Court—therefore hurry up." Obviously, he feared illegal publication.

As the Leipzig publisher issued, besides the original edition, an arrangement for 2 Violins, 2 Violas and Violoncello, announced on August 18th, 1802, and not admitted to be a transcription, since the title merely said "Quintette", Beethoven, towards the end of October, 1802, felt himself bound to proclaim openly that this was an original Quintet by himself. His pupil, Ferdinand Ries[1]), maintains that this Quintet arrangement emanated from Beethoven. On the other hand this is true of the trans-cription for Piano, Clarinet or Violin and Violoncello which appeared as Beethoven's op. 38 on November 8th, 1803. The composer dedicated this to his doctor, Johann Adam Schmidt, whose family was musical; and, according to the custom of the time, the doctor remained in possession of the manuscript for a year. In this trans-cription, which is very pianistic, passages specially suitable to the horn do not emerge particularly successfully.

For a lengthy and uncommonly able study of this Septet we are indebted to Hermann Deiters in the second edition of the second volume of Alexander Wheelock Thayer's "Ludwig van Beethoven's Leben" (edited and supplemented by Hugo Riemann, 1910). There, strangely enough, Mozart's D major Divertimento (Köchel Nº 334) is accepted as the model for our Septet as having the same arrangement of movements; but this is not a fitting comparison[2]), even if the Mozart Variations were imitated in key and general form. It is known that the composer borrowed the Menuett from his little Piano Sonata, op. 49, Nº 2 (written in 1792), but handled it independently. The theme on which the variations are founded has been traced to a folk-song of the Lower Rhine ("Ach Schiffer, lieber Schiffer") which Andr. Kretzschmer published in his "German Folk-songs" (1838). But Zuccalmaglio seems to have provided the words to Beethoven's music. As Heinrich Rietsch truthfullys says in his "Kurze Betrachtungen zum deutschen Volkslied", in the recently published review comme-morating the 90th birth-day of Rochus Freiherr von Liliencron (page 222)—as long as it remains unproved that the classically treated theme existed before Beethoven as a folk-song, he must be considered the originator.

For the purposes of the present re-print, which only differs from the older edition in having 14 staves per page instead of 21, Beethoven's original score has been studied and compared in some passages—a score which, as a present from the Mendelssohn-Bartholdy family, has lain since April, 1909, in the Music Collection of the Imperial Library at Berlin.

Wilh. Altmann

---

[1]) Wegeler & Ries, "Biographial Notes on Ludwig van Beethoven", New impression by Kalischer (1906) page 112.
[2]) It would be more just to bring forward for comparison Mozart's Divertimento for String Trio in E flat major (Köchel No. 563). But even here the introduction to the first and last movement is lacking.

BEETHOVEN, SEPTETT ESDUR, OP. 20

Beethovens Septett, wohl sein populärstes, in zahllosen Arrangements ver-
breitetes, von ihm später deswegen etwas unterschätztes Werk, kann in motivischer
Hinsicht teilweise auf das noch aus der Bonner Zeit des Komponisten stammende
Sextett für 2 Klarinetten, 2 Hörner und 2 Fagotte (veröffentlicht als op. 71) zurück-
geführt werden. Skizzen zu dem Septett stammen aus dem Jahre 1799. Nachdem
es zuerst in einer Privatsoiree beim Fürsten Schwarzenberg zu Gehör gekommen
war, wurde es öffentlich in einem Konzert Beethovens am 2. April 1800 im Kaiser-
lich-Königlichen National-Hoftheater in Wien aufgeführt. In der Ankündigung
dieses Konzertes steht bereits, daß dieses Septett der Kaiserin Maria Theresia[1]), der
zweiten Gemahlin des Kaisers Franz II., gewidmet ist. Erst am 15. Dezember 1800
bot der Komponist es dem Verleger Franz Anton Hoffmeister an, der kurz zuvor
mit dem Organisten Ambrosius Kühnel in Leipzig das „Bureau de Musique" (seit
1814 C. F. Peters) gegründet hatte. In diesem Briefe bezeichnet er die einzelnen
Stimmen sämtlich als obligat und fährt dann fort: „ich kann gar nichts unobligates
schreiben, weil ich schon mit einem obligaten Accompagnement auf die Welt gekommen bin. Dieses Septett hat sehr gefallen. Zum häufigen Gebrauch könnte
man die 3 Blasinstrumente, nämlich Fagotto[2]), Clarinetto und Corno in noch eine
Violine, noch eine Viola und noch ein Violoncello übersetzen[3])." Als Honorar ver-
langt er dann am 15. Januar 1801 dasselbe wie für die erste Symphonie op. 21 und
für die Klavier-Sonate op. 22, nämlich 20 Dukaten, was er auch offenbar erhalten
hat. Im Juni 1801 versichert er dann seinen Verlegern, die durch ein Gerücht
stutzig geworden waren, daß er ihnen ausschließlich diese Werke verkauft habe,
und fügt hinzu: „übrigens glaube ich ebenso wenig, daß Salomon[4]) eines so
schlechten Streichs, das Septett stechen zu lassen, fähig ist, als ich, es ihm verkauft zu haben; ich bin so gewissenhaft, daß ich verschiedenen Verlegern den
Klavier-Auszug von dem Septett, um den sie mich angesucht haben, abgeschlagen, und
doch weiß ich nicht einmal, ob Sie auf diese Art Gebrauch davon machen werden".
In demselben Briefe gab Beethoven folgenden Titel für das Septett in der heute
uns sonderbar vorkommenden Schreibweise an:

Septette

Pour un violon., Viole, violon celle, contre Basse, un cors, une Clarinette, un fagot
composé et dedié
à Sa. Majesté l'imperatrice et Reine
par louis van Beethoven
œuvre 20.

Auf dem Titelblatt der in zwei Teilen ausgegebenen Originalausgabe, die erst
um die Mitte des Jahres 1802 erschienen zu sein scheint. steht aber: „Septetto

---

[1]) Vgl. über diese 1807 nach der Geburt ihres zwölften Kindes im Alter von 34 Jahren ge-
storbene Kaiserin Carl Leeder, Beethovens Widmungen in: Die Musik, Bd. 10 (1904), S. 425 f.
[2]) Man beachte die merkwürdige Reihenfolge der entsprechenden Instrumente.
[3]) Merkwürdigerweise ist gerade dieses Arrangement nicht erschienen; dagegen kam ein anderes,
das Beethoven seinem Leipziger Verleger am 22. April 1801 empfiehlt, nämlich für Flötenquintett
(d. h. für Flöte, Violine, 2 Bratschen und Violoncell), transponiert nach G dur, bei Witzendorf in
Wien heraus. „Dadurch würde den Flötenliebhabern, die mich schon darum angegangen, geholfen,
und sie würden darin wie die Insekten herumschwärmen und daran speisen" schreibt Beethoven
in diesem Briefe.
[4]) Diesem bekannten Konzertveranstalter in London hatte Beethoven aus Freundschaft das
Septett geschickt, ehe er es an Hoffmeister gesandt, um es in London aufführen zu lassen, aber
mit der ausdrücklichen Weisung, es ja nicht in andere Hände kommen zu lassen, weil er es in
Deutschland stechen lassen wolle.

pour Violon, Alto, Clarinette, Corno, Basson, Violoncelle et Contre-Basse composé et dedié à Sa Majesté Marie Therese, L'Imperatrice romaine, Reine d'Hongrie et de Bohème etc. etc. par Louis van Beethoven. Oeuvre 20."

Am 8. April 1802 mahnte Beethoven die Verleger zur rascheren Veröffentlichung des Septetts folgendermaßen: „mein Septett schickt ein wenig geschwinder in die Welt — weil der Pöbel drauf harrt, und Ihr wißts, die Kaiserin hats — und Lumpe gibts in der Kaiserlichen Stadt wie am Kaiserlichen Hof — ich stehe Euch darin für nichts gut — darum spudet Euch.ª Offenbar fürchtete er eine unrechtmäßige Veröffentlichung.

Da der Leipziger Verlag neben der Original-Ausgabe ein Arrangement des Septetts für 2 Violinen, 2 Bratschen und Violoncello erscheinen ließ, die bereits am 18. August 1802 angezeigt wurde und gar nicht als Bearbeitung gekennzeichnet war, indem der Titel nur „Quintetteª lautete, sah sich Beethoven gegen Ende Oktober 1802 gezwungen, öffentlich dagegen zu protestieren, daß dies ein Originalquintett von ihm sei. Sein Schüler Ferdinand Ries[1]) behauptet freilich, daß dieses Quintett-Arrangement von Beethoven selbst herrührt. Dagegen ist dies der Fall bei der Bearbeitung für Klavier, Klarinette oder Violine und Violoncell, die als Beethovens op. 38 zuerst am 8. November 1803 angezeigt ist. Der Komponist widmete sie seinem Arzt Dr. Johann Adam Schmidt, der in seiner Familie viel Musik machte, und ließ ihn der damaligen Sitte gemäß ein Jahr im Besitz des Manuskriptes. Die spezifischen Hornpassagen kommen in dieser Bearbeitung, die sehr klaviergerecht ist, natürlich nicht besonders zur Geltung.

Eine ungemein zutreffende längere Charakteristik dieses Septetts verdanken wir Hermann Deiters in der zweiten Auflage des zweiten Bandes von Alexander Wheelock Thayers „Ludwig van Beethovens Lebenª (herausgegeben und ergänzt von Hugo Riemann 1910). Dort ist merkwürdigerweise Mozarts D dur-Divertimento (Köchel No. 334) als Vorbild für unser Septett angenommen, weil es dieselbe Ordnung der Sätze haben soll, was aber gar nicht[2]) zutrifft, wie denn auch die Mozartschen Variationen in ihrer Tonart und Bewegung nachgebildet sein sollen. Daß das Menuett vom Komponisten seiner kleinen Klavier-Sonate op. 49 No. 2 (komponiert 1796) entnommen, aber selbständig behandelt ist, ist bekannt. In dem den Variationen zugrunde liegenden Thema wollte man ein niederrheinisches Volkslied („Ach Schiffer, lieber Schifferª) erblicken, das Andr. Kretzschmer in seinen „Deutschen Volksliedernª (1838) veröffentlicht hat. Allein Zuccalmaglio scheint der Beethovenschen Melodie erst den Text untergelegt zu haben. Mit Recht sagt daher Heinrich Rietsch („Kurze Betrachtungen zum deutschen Volksliedª in der kürzlich erschienenen Festschrift zum 90. Geburtstag von Rochus Freiherrn von Liliencron S. 222), so lange nicht der Nachweis geführt ist, daß das klassizistisch geführte Thema vor Beethoven als Volkslied vorkommt, habe er für den Erfinder zu gelten.

Für die vorliegende Neuausgabe, die sich von ihrer Vorgängerin darin unterscheidet, daß jetzt nur 14 Linien auf der Seite gegen 21 stehen, ist an einigen Stellen die Original-Partitur Beethovens verglichen worden, die als Geschenk der Familie von Mendelssohn-Bartholdy seit April 1909 in der Musiksammlung der Königlichen Bibliothek zu Berlin sich befindet.

Wilh. Altmann

---

[1]) Wegeler & Ries, Biographische Notizen über Ludwig van Beethoven. Neudruck von Kalischer (1906) S. 112.
[2]) Eher könnte man das Divertimento Mozarts für Streichtrio (Köchel No. 563) in Es dur zum Vergleich heranziehen. Aber auch hier fehlt die Einleitung zum ersten und letzten Satz.

SEPTET

I.

L. van Beethoven, Op. 20.
1770-1827

E.E.1112

Ernst Eulenburg Ltd

4

8

E.E. 1112

14

B.E.1112

II.

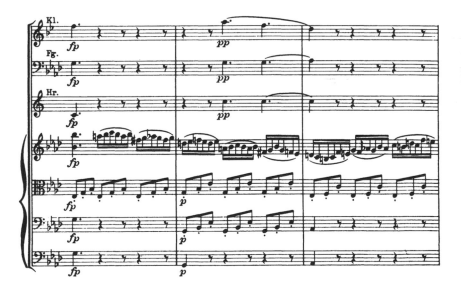

82

E.E.1112

84

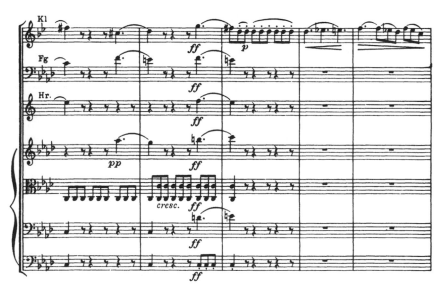

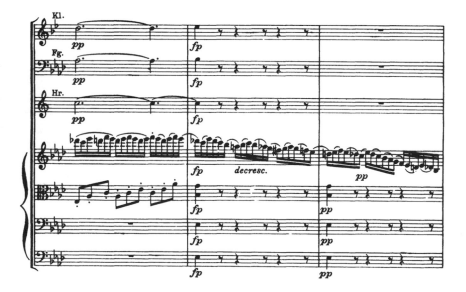

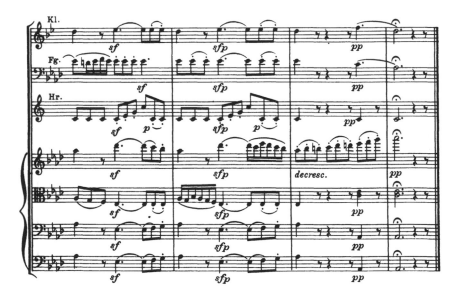

III.

Tempo di Menuetto. ♩ = 120

Trio.

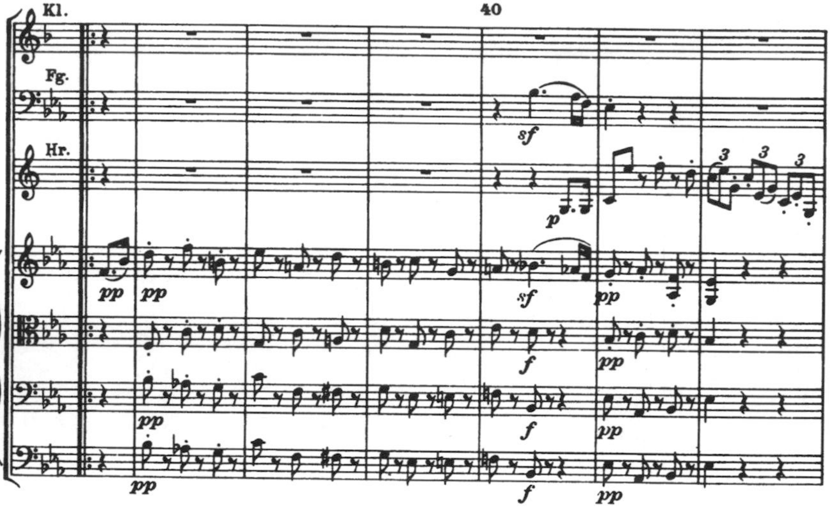
Kl.
Fg.
Hr.
40
pp
sf
f
p

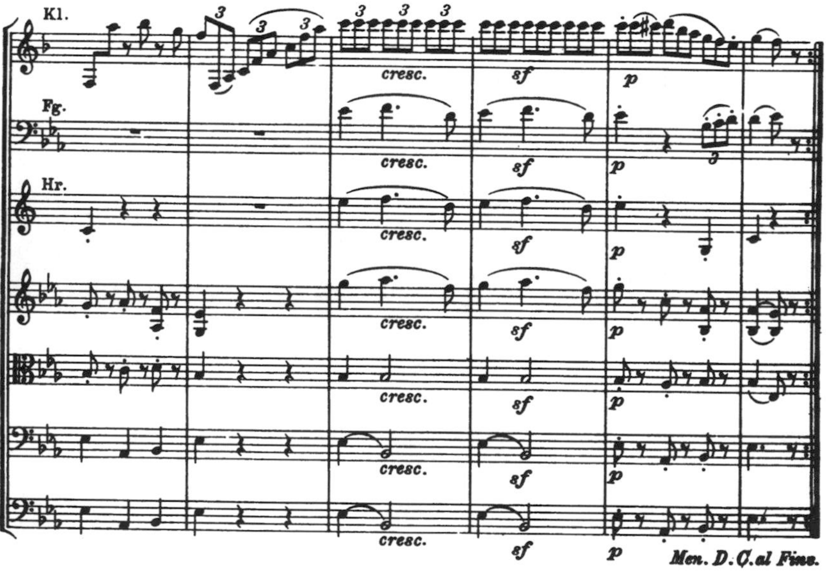
Kl.
Fg.
Hr.
cresc.
sf
p
Men. D.C. al Fine.

IV.

Tema con Variazioni. Andante. ♪ = 120

46

Var. I.

E. E. 1112

48

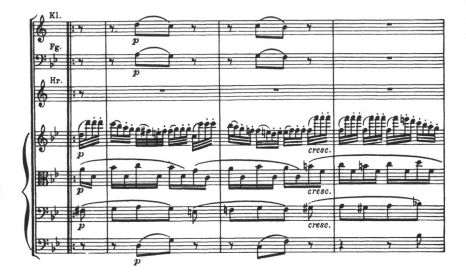

Var. III.

Var. IV.

Var. V.

V.

Scherzo. Allegro molto e vivace. ♩=126

58

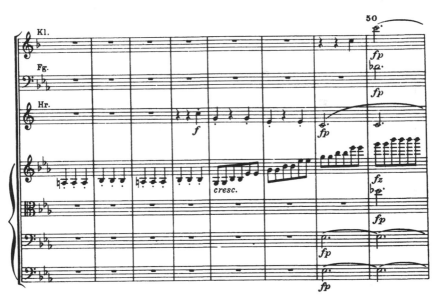

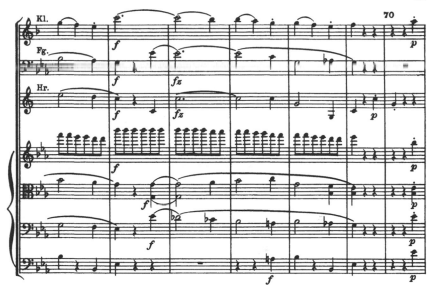

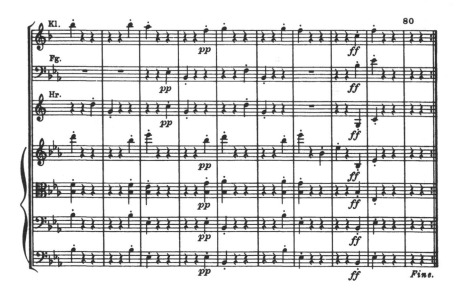

Trio.

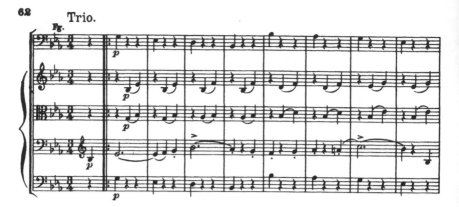

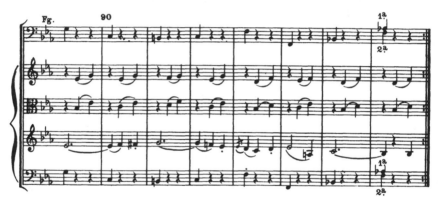

Scherzo D. C.
al Fine.

VI.

Andante con moto alla Marcia. ♪=76

68

E.E.1112

82